T0209404

GRACIE'S CROSSING

A SPIRITUAL JOURNEY

RON MATTHEW FRAZIER

iUniverse

GRACIE'S CROSSING
A SPIRITUAL JOURNEY

iUniverse books may be ordered through booksellers or by contacting:

iUniverse
1663 Liberty Drive
Bloomington, IN 47403
www.iuniverse.com
844-349-9409

ISBN: 978-1-6632-5300-2 (sc)
ISBN: 978-1-6632-5421-4 (e)

Library of Congress Control Number: 2023912123

Print information available on the last page.

iUniverse rev. date: 06/22/2023

In memory of my mother, Effie

❧ CONTENTS

Preface ix
Acknowledgments. xi

Chapter 1   Knowing Gracie. .1
Chapter 2   Gracie's Siblings. .7
Chapter 3   COVID-19 Lockdown 10
Chapter 4   Contacting the Psychic 13
Chapter 5   Our Last Days Together 17
Chapter 6   A Day of Grace. 20
Chapter 7   A Graceful Exit. 24
Chapter 8   Making It Known 31
Chapter 9   A Visit from the Psychic 34

Afterword 41

❧ PREFACE

For some time now, I have wanted to tell a story, the true story of my rescue dog Gracie and the experiences we had near the end of her life. So many of us have gone through the pain of losing our beloved four-legged family members, and that pain and uncertainty can be devastating. Too many of us, I believe, have never been taught how to understand this grief or find a source of refuge and reassurance.

In writing this book, I have wanted to share a wonderful, majestic, emotional, epic, and highly spiritual experience. The thought of the last days we had with Gracie brings me great peace. It is my sincerest hope that those of us who know that pain all too well will get the same comfort or even just a moment of peace and insight. It is especially important to me that readers of this story get to know Gracie's personality and her silliness—maybe this story will help elicit a smile when you think of your family pet members who have crossed over, and maybe even provide some comfort when the time comes for you to say goodbye.

The book was inspired by the journal I was encouraged to keep by my therapist. After Gracie had crossed, my emotions were deep, and I found myself struggling every day to process the loss of her. I had panic attacks at three in the morning. I couldn't sleep, and when I did find rest, it was usually short. I asked my personal physician about a therapist who specialized in grief counseling.

My therapist encouraged me to start journaling my feelings, emotions, and details about the experience. The goal was to express the emotions so that during our sessions we could unpack them and work through them. The journal was emotional and cathartic. Reliving the pain I had experienced with Gracie as she made her exit brought me to tears again. I give my therapist much credit for rescuing me with one simple phrase: "Grief is not linear!" Once the journal was completed and I read back over it, I was helped so very much by seeing the story of Gracie's crossing in written form. There was a beautiful story on those pages.

I have shared this story with many of my friends who went through losses with their own family pets, and each time it made me realize this story not only helped me with my grief, but helped those that I shared her story with as well. So the journal became a manuscript, and the manuscript now becomes a book. This is how *Gracie's Crossing* was born.

❧ ACKNOWLEDGMENTS

I would be remiss not to thank the people who contributed in some way or inspired me to write this book. I sought and received guidance from those here on the earth and from those ancestors who have passed. I have dedicated this book to my mother, who physically left this planet over thirty years ago but who never misses an opportunity to let me know she is always watching and still here with me in spirit. Without a doubt, Mom, you send obvious signs and signals from the heavens to let me know I am on the right path. Without you, I would not have made it this far. Before the book was completed, my niece Rhonda crossed over, and I truly believe she helped motivate me in ways that I can only describe as a heavenly intervention.

I would also like to thank the friends who helped me right after Gracie crossed over. Sharon, Lindsey, and Wanda, all of you were always available, day or night, to talk me down off the ledge and listen to me pour out my heart. Thank you for listening! I knew you understood this pain. Thank you also to my friends Rick and Peter, who were always happy to doggy-sit when I needed them. And thank you to the Lopez family, my adopted family, for taking Gracie during a rough time when she needed to be kept safe. She made fast friends with her canine sisters Snowball and Bella, and I know how much you loved her!

I am kept in a constant state of amusement and unconditional love by my sidekick and constant shadow, Rico, and my three kitties, Duey, Izzy, and Phoenix. They give me strength and purpose. I'm so thankful they are in my life!

And finally, to Gracie: I never could have imagined how much you would change my life. Your life also changed my spirit. You truly were sent by God as an angel. You watched over all of us while you were here, and you are watching over us still. I am quite certain you have become our guardian angel. You taught me lessons I did not know I needed to learn. You taught me about myself, and most of all you taught me patience and how to love unconditionally. I love you to the heavens and back. I cannot wait to see you again in heaven! Thank you for loving us.

CHAPTER 1
KNOWING GRACIE

Gracie was brought to me by what I can only see as a sign from the universe. I was living in Van Nuys with my little furry kid and companion, Rico, who was still a puppy at five years old. Rico is half Chihuahua, half Jack Russell, and at times all tornado! His markings often cause people to mistake him for a miniature Siberian husky. There were two other dogs in the house at the time, both golden retrievers belonging to my friend George, which made for a home full of high energy, shenanigans, and laughs.

The day Gracie came waltzing down the sidewalk seemed ordinary, but now that I look back, it was the beginning of a life-changing experience I will always cherish. It was also an experience that would teach me things about death and dying, emotion, love, and the other dimension—the beyond. Those of us who believe in an afterlife, or the next dimension, may call this place heaven. Others simply call it "the other side."

Gracie was a corgi mix with black and brown markings and short little legs. She was quite stocky, around thirty pounds or so. She was a drop-off in our neighborhood. By "drop-off," I mean a pet dropped off by someone who cannot or does not want to care for their pet any longer. A small dog park at the end of our street was known as a place where people came to leave their animals behind, as it was secure and many dog parents visited there to play. I saw it happen far too often, but usually an animal lover soon scooped up the abandoned pets and took them home. There are better ways to surrender an animal, but I will assume they hoped a drop-off has a better chance of rescue than at a shelter. As much as I wish this practice would stop, in this case it worked out because it brought me Gracie.

On this day, as soon as George came home from work, he asked if I knew that a little dog was on our front walk. I did not. I went out to the walk and saw this very friendly creature, her tail wagging. I knew everyone in the neighborhood and their dogs, and I had never seen her before. I brought her inside for food and water. She had no collar and was not chipped. Then I went back outside with her to see if anyone else might recognize her. I saw the mail carrier a few doors down and asked if he knew where she lived. He confirmed that she had been dropped off several days ago—he had seen the car leave her behind and drive away. At that moment, I knew she was mine. My humanity simply took over. It was clear that this dog needed to have a loving home and to feel safe.

I remember that day well because it was my late mother's birthday, May 24, and now this date would become Gracie's "birthday" as well. I had been in a weird mood all day. Short-tempered, almost agitated, but not sure why my mood was so down. After I was able to get Gracie settled, I spoke to my sister over the phone and told her about the dog. She reminded me that it was our mother's birthday. We both giggled and thought it was just one of many signs I have received from our mother over the years after she crossed. She was always up to something, sending me messages in one form or another, but this time, she sent me a dog!

The newcomer to the household was given the name Grace, because many of my friends thought she looked like she could be Rico's mommy, whose name was Grace. (His papa's name was Digger.) Strangely, she responded to this name almost immediately. It seemed fitting: an angel sent from heaven by my mother *should* be called Grace. Although Grace was her formal name, her nickname became Gracie. She was Grace when she was in trouble, and Gracie when she was being silly. Rico and Grace bonded and became fast companions—a relationship I would greatly miss, as he would too, once she was gone.

Gracie came with special needs. She was diagnosed with Cushing's disease, which, I learned, can present as an eating disorder. Cushing's caused her never to feel full. It causes dogs to eat until they cannot eat any longer, which in turn can cause illness or even death. At feeding time, Gracie would try to bully the other animals in the house for their food. She would push the kitties out of the way and scarf down their kibble or salmon, bowl by bowl, and then turn back to her own food dish. She was never mean about it, but she was a stubborn one when it came to food. The kitties would let her eat their food, then look at me to give them more. After her diagnosis, we had to limit her food intake and make sure she ate just her own food. I started feeding the kitties up on the table so Gracie couldn't get to their dishes. It was a constant job, and often she grabbed the other dogs' treats and the kitties' treats!

There were times she made even bolder attempts at taking human food, and often succeeded. Always the character, believe me! One incident still brings a smile to my face. I had cooked dinner and grilled a steak outside. Having made my plate, I placed it on the coffee table. (Yes, I like to eat in front of the TV, but who doesn't?) I went to the kitchen to grab a napkin and more ice for my drink. When I came back to sit down to eat, I noticed there was something quite different about my dinner plate. The steak had vanished!

Hmm. I looked around the room, checked the floor, even looked under the coffee table. No steak!

I went back outside to check the grill, thinking that maybe I hadn't even brought it inside, but the grill was empty. I looked at Rico. "Hey, booboo, have you seen my steak?" I knew Rico would never take food from my plate. He always waited to see if it was something he would like before giving me those sad eyes and guilting me into sharing a bite. I honestly did not know where it could have disappeared to and had to laugh, but then I had my aha moment: Gracie!

I looked around the room for her, but she was nowhere in sight. I took myself on a little expedition down the hallway and into the back bedrooms. Although I didn't see her or my steak, I heard the chomping noise of someone eating very hurriedly and thoroughly enjoying whatever they were eating. I walked over and looked under the bed. There she was, with a steak bone in her mouth and steak all over her face. That look on her face was priceless, as if she were saying, "What are you looking at? I didn't do anything, and I don't know anything about any steak."

Trying not to laugh, I said in a stern voice, "Grace! What have you done?" She dropped the bone and came out with her tail between her legs, knowing she had not done a good thing and doing her best to show some remorse. I felt so guilty *she* felt guilt that I started laughing and could not contain myself. Grace hit the hallway running with her tail in full wag mode and went right back to the original scene of the crime.

I walked back to where I had planned to eat my dinner and sat down to my potatoes and green beans, then looked over at Gracie. "I'm not sure what you want now, Missy, because you've taken the best part of my dinner, but I plan on eating the rest myself." The steak story is one of my favorites.

Gracie always knew she was loved and protected. But she didn't like it when I wasn't in her view (unless she was on the run with a stolen treat, or my steak!), and she had an obvious fear of riding in the car. Car rides with her seemed to give her great anxiety. She would pant and sometimes whimper. I believe it was related to the way she was dropped off by her previous family. She never really got used to car rides. Taking her to my family on holidays or to the dog beach was upsetting to her, though once she arrived at our destination, she was okay and playful.

One day my friend Tanner and I took Rico and Gracie to the dog beach to spend the day. Gracie loved the water. She was too short to get too far in, but she would go to the water's edge and roll around and end up covered in sand. Rico, on the other hand, isn't a water dog at all. He would follow her to the shoreline and watch her roll around. I often wondered what he was thinking as he sat there and watched. Maybe he enjoyed watching her be silly as much as we humans did.

As we were sitting on our beach towels and watching the dogs run and play, I asked Tanner to keep an eye on them so I could get us something to drink from the concession stand. I had paid and was waiting to get the drinks when I saw Tanner running across the beach. He was yelling Gracie's name and repeating "Stop! Stop!" I wasn't sure what was up until I saw Gracie forty to fifty feet in front of him, running as fast as those little corgi legs would go, towards the parking lot. He finally caught up with her, picked her up, and carried her back to our spot on the towels.

I grabbed our drinks and headed back to them. Gracie spotted me as soon as I came into view and started running towards me. She looked so excited to see me. Tanner said that when Gracie had come up from the water and realized I wasn't there on the towels, she took off towards the parking lot, looking for me and visibly upset when she couldn't find me. I didn't realize how much attention she paid to me until that moment.

From that day forward, whenever we went to the dog beach, to keep her calm I always made sure she had a direct view of me. And I always had to keep an eye on her. Many times she approached other beachgoers, warmed her way into their space, and before they knew it had something of theirs in her mouth. She was great at getting people to let their guard down, and then she would snag their sandwiches or chips and make a mad dash back to her spot. I guess she thought she wouldn't be in trouble if she made it back to her towel or to me. She was quite a character, and we had many moments like this during our time together.

CHAPTER 2
GRACIE'S SIBLINGS

Gracie and Rico, who as I write is close to the ripe old age of eighteen, were inseparable for her entire life. But our little family has also had feline members.

Duey is an enormous tabby cat, a rescue from a friend who couldn't care for him any longer because of his work situation. So I adopted him, broken leg and all, and moved him into my growing family. He weighs eighteen pounds.

At the time I worked in renewable energy and spent a lot of time in other people's homes and businesses. One client's cat had recently given birth to a litter of five kittens. This one kitten in particular would not leave me alone while I was trying to work. My clients, who were calling the kitten Oreo, because of her black and white markings, kept telling me I should adopt her. When I arrived at their home for meetings, they often had this kitten sitting in my chair. Clearly, these clients knew me well and were playing on my love of animals. After one of our project meetings, I was driving home and couldn't rid my mind of the image of that kitten sitting in my lap during our presentation. I got off the freeway, turned around, and headed back to their home. They were waiting for me with the kitten in their hands. "I knew you'd be back," my client Linda said. So I brought home a new member to join my family, which was now at four. But I knew I wasn't going to keep that name Oreo, and gave her the name Izzy. She's a gorgeous cat.

The baby of our family I named Phoenix. He was rescued after a neighbor alerted me to a high-pitched squeak coming from my backyard. I had heard the sound the day before, but it sounded like a bird, and I didn't give it further thought. Little did I know that it was—at the bottom of a nine-foot hole the city had dug for a new sewer line—a tiny feral kitten. It was around one in the morning when I found him, but I took him to the closest emergency vet hospital and got him checked out. The vet estimated his age at around three weeks. During the drive home, I declared his name: "Phoenix!" The name fit a survivor like him perfectly.

Phoenix has become one of my greatest joys, and he warmed his way into Gracie's heart from day one. That night when I introduced Phoenix to the group, Gracie was the first one to run up to him and lick his face. She assumed the role of big sister right away. I told myself that Gracie must have sensed they were both orphans. They had a wonderful and sweet relationship. Phoenix is extremely playful, and he especially loved to play with Gracie. He would wait, usually up on some piece of furniture, for her to walk past him. Then from above, he would take his front paw and swipe at her back or butt. As soon as he made contact, he would take off running. It was fun to watch, and Gracie would try to get to him, but her short corgi legs could never catch up. But she did her best, and at bedtime I would find those two snuggled up, usually with Phoenix passed out on top of Gracie. She didn't seem to mind. I think she loved it, to be honest!

Still, Gracie's relationship with Rico was the strongest. They did everything together. A trip to the mailbox was always with both Rico and Gracie. Trips to my family's house always included Rico and

Gracie. They were the grandkids—four-legged grandkids! —always welcomed there and always loved.

Duey and Izzy didn't engage with Gracie as Rico and Phoenix did, but they were aware of Gracie and loved her. They had a respectful relationship based on mutual trust. I never saw them fight or bicker. They would pass each other in the house or the yard and just do their own thing.

CHAPTER 3

COVID-19 LOCKDOWN

COVID-19 put many of us in strange places and strange situations. I was stranded back east in early February of 2020 with my four-legged gang. We were in a rental home and isolated like everyone else, but I also had to earn a living. I took a job as an assistant store manager for a big chain store to help as best I could, since so many people were afraid to come out and the workforce was suffering a shortage.

It was around August of that year that Gracie started to decline. She no longer scarfed up any food left unguarded; in fact, she seemed to have lost interest in food. Remember, she had a compulsive eating disorder, and for her not to eat was a bad sign. I took her to the closest vet and had her medical records sent over from our vet in California. They saw the diagnosis of Cushing's disease and explained that it could be the tumor from the disease causing her loss of appetite. I knew we were in trouble, and I knew that this would be a challenging time in my life.

I was working more than forty hours a week. During lockdown, as many of us remember, businesses that were open had strict requirements for monitoring employees' temperature and symptoms. One night not long after Gracie's vet visit, when I was the manager on duty, I went to the health desk for my temperature check and found that it was 104! I notified the other off-duty managers that I was headed to the emergency room. At the ER, I had a temperature of 105.2, but the attending physician would not admit me because the high temperature was my only symptom.

This event sent my life, my faith, and my physical and mental health all into a tailspin. I was nervous and scared. I had to wait for the test results, because at the beginning of the pandemic, no rapid testing was available. I had to isolate and wait. When the test results came in a few days, I was positive. I was terrified, but I also knew that I had my little animal family to care for, especially Gracie. But everything happens for a reason, though I didn't know it at the time.

I believe I contracted COVID that August so I could spend time and bond with Gracie, whose health was quickly deteriorating. My diagnosis and having to stay isolated at home gave me time off not only to recuperate but to get to know Gracie even better. Watching her interact with her siblings and with me twenty-four hours a day, I learned how gentle her soul was and how caring she was. I saw her relationship with the other animals in detail, their actions and relationships with one another, how they snuggled up and napped together. Rico would share his treats with Gracie, even though she didn't seem interested. And even with her health declining, Gracie always did her best to check on me. She followed me from room to room and sat next to me every chance she got, bonding even more deeply to me during my illness.

Before I left work with COVID-19, a coworker had handed me a business card. She thought it might be a valuable resource for Gracie, should we need help. The card had the number and website for a well-known animal psychic in the area. I did not know it at the time, but this contact would forever alter my fear of death, and more important, lift me up out of the tailspin my life took after Gracie crossed.

CHAPTER 4

CONTACTING THE PSYCHIC

August ran into September. With each day that passed, Gracie declined. It sounded like she was struggling to breathe, and she had no desire for food, except for certain cat treats that I made sure were always available. When I showered, she would hide under the bed in our bedroom. I had never seen her do this, and I wondered whether she didn't want the other animals to know she was sick. Gracie had now been with me for eight and a half years, and vets had estimated her age at around eleven. I could see that her body weight was dropping, and she slept more and more. This was the end stage of her disease; I was told by the local vet. She was not in pain, but I could tell we were getting close to either losing her on her own time or making the call to help her with hospice vet care.

Not aware of any local vets who made house calls for this procedure, I remembered the card given to me by my coworker. I have never been involved in euthanizing an animal. I didn't know how it worked or what to expect. I had to dig deep. I did a lot of praying and asking for guidance. I wasn't sure if this was the right choice for Gracie. One thing for certain, Gracie's last ride would not be in the car to the vet. Her fear of cars had never subsided.

Since I have always assumed this fear arose from her former family dropping her off and driving away, I didn't want to force her to ride in the car to the vet's office and have her last moments away from her family. It was heartbreaking.

By the second week of September, Gracie's decline had become very noticeable. She was able to walk and drink water, but she had limited energy. She could take short limited walks outside, but her weight was dropping and her breathing was more and more labored. I found the psychic's card and made the call. She was truly kind, very calm. She told me she was super busy, especially because of COVID. She provided a list of local vets who made hospice home visits. She suggested I call right away to get Gracie scheduled.

The animal psychic asked me for a short video and a current picture of Gracie. After she received the video and picture, she responded right away with a text that simply read *She's almost ready to go* and told me to act fast. I was able to contact a few of the hospice vets and waited for a return call to see if they could fit us in their schedule.

The following day I received a call from the psychic. We spoke about the process of euthanasia and what I should expect. She said that it happens very quickly, usually in about five minutes. The procedure would involve two injections, one to relax them and the second to stop the heart. I worried the procedure itself would cause Gracie pain. I listened as she told me over and over that when there is suffering, this is the more humane thing to do. She said she would try to be there when it was time for Gracie to pass, depending on her schedule. I asked more questions about the procedure, and then we began to speak about things of a more spiritual nature.

The psychic answered each question calmly and with confidence in her voice. She assured me that from her years of experience, she knew that once these beloved creatures were released from the physical body, they would find the "light," and then the light would guide them to the next dimension. There is a release, and there is no more pain. She also spoke about the journey. It would take Gracie three days to cross over. I was not to worry, because they know they are safe and surrounded by love. They are alone on their journey, but they are not afraid. I needed more reassurance regarding pain from the procedure of euthanasia, and she said that no animal had ever told her about experiencing any pain. It is a normal release of their spirit and energy. There is only freedom. They are always incredibly grateful to be released and pain-free. She shared these insights with me in absolute confidence.

Honestly, the only concern from our conversation that I could not justify in my own thoughts and in my heart was the taking three days to cross. I did not want Gracie to be on her own without me for three days. I did not mention this to the psychic. I didn't mention this to anyone but Gracie. I could not wrap my head around her being alone without me to protect her during her journey, even though I knew she was going home to her ultimate destination. But I had my faith. It would have to be enough.

By the third week of September, Gracie was holding on, but I knew I couldn't let her continue. My heart broke watching this beautiful creature deteriorate and struggle. She wasn't eating anything at all and was barely drinking water. She couldn't walk on her own and could stand for only a few seconds.

I made an appointment at the local vet's office and scheduled her for Wednesday, September 23, 2020, at 5:00 p.m. This would be her last visit, and it would end her pain. It was the hardest call I have ever made in my life. It was unbearable, the thought of taking her in the car to this appointment. I prayed. I made calls to several of the local hospice vets that the animal psychic had given to me, but they were all booked because of the pandemic. I kept calling the hospice vets, hoping one would become available. One did call back but couldn't be there for another week. I knew that was too long for her.

Having COVID made it even more difficult. Although I was on the tail end of the virus, I still had a few mild symptoms. I was worried that if I couldn't get a hospice vet to our house, COVID wouldn't allow me to be with Gracie at the vet's office. It was an impossible situation. I dreaded taking her by car to the vet for the euthanasia appointment we had scheduled, and I might not even get to be with her because of the Covid restrictions.

I remember looking at her and telling her that it was almost over. But our current path's ending was breaking my heart. Even though I wasn't sure I was doing the right thing, I knew it would take a miracle for her to stay with us. That miracle never came. I realize now that what came from this experience was a different miracle. One that would end her pain and set her free. And one that would allow me to see things I could never have imagined were possible.

CHAPTER 5
OUR LAST DAYS TOGETHER

During the last few weeks of Gracie's illness, I moved us all into the family room, where we all slept on the sectional sofa together. Before, we had slept in the master bedroom, sharing a king-size bed. I tend to sleep on my side and was usually trapped in the middle, surrounded by Rico on one side, Gracie down by my feet, Izzy next to my head, and Phoenix behind my knees. Duey slept on the chair beside the bed. But Gracie couldn't get up or down from the bed because it was too tall, so my solution was to move us to the sectional in the family room, which was lower to the floor. We had to be together and close to Gracie. I didn't want to leave her side for a second. I did not want her to be alone if her life ended.

Rico, the cats, and I all seemed to share some unspoken agreement that we would take turns sleeping in short shifts. Each one of us took time to sit next to her and show her the love she deserved. I watched Rico jump on the sofa next to her while she rested on her favorite blanket. He looked directly at her, and she lay on her blanket watching him back, as if they were communicating. Of course, there were no words I could hear, but I felt in my heart they were having their last talk. They sat beside each other and did not move for a long while. When Rico finally went to lie in his spot on the sofa, Gracie raised her head a couple of times to look after him. I knew she loved Rico and didn't want to say goodbye. Not to him. Not to any of us.

Izzy and Duey each took their turn sitting next to her over the next seventy-two hours, and over these three days it seemed that everyone had said their goodbyes. Almost everyone—I hadn't taken my turn, and neither had Phoenix.

I didn't sleep much that week, but I tried to take care of myself as best I could because I wanted to be coherent if she needed me. Still, I was worn out from the effects of COVID and from worrying about Gracie. We were all tired. But this was for Gracie. I was willing to sacrifice sleep and chores around the house to make sure she was not alone. She had brought us so much love over the last eight and a half years. We needed to show her that even in her last hours, our love was strong. And the truth is that our love had grown stronger. Knowing you love someone is the easy part. The hard part is knowing that the amount of love you have will equal the amount of pain and grief when they leave.

I would later learn of this balance during my grief therapy. My therapist put it like this: the measure of your love for someone will be the measure of your grief. That makes perfect sense to me. I knew that I loved this creature unconditionally and felt a paternal need to protect her until the very end and even beyond.

The animal psychic checked in on us a few times and asked for pictures of Gracie. The last one I sent to her brought an immediate and very direct response: *She is ready to go, let her go!* Gracie's siblings were all in the room, watching me with her. I told them it was okay. Gracie was going to be okay. They all seemed to be hanging on my every word and every action, as if they were in a trance. None of them moved.

It was now Tuesday. After I hung up with the psychic, I looked at Gracie and told her I was ready. "It is okay for you to go." Tears flooded my cheeks. I had to wipe them away just to be able to see her face. I told her I loved her and thanked her for coming to us, saying again, "It's okay. You can go now."

Memories flooded my brain. I thought about the day she came into my life after being abandoned. I remembered the time she looked for me at the beach and how she was so upset that she tried to run back to the car to find me. Stealing my steak and hiding with it. Chasing Phoenix all over the house. The holiday visits to my family's house in Rialto and how she loved being there with everyone. All the times I had to carry her outside and back when she was getting so weak. I loved that she needed me, and I knew I was going to miss this oh-so-very-much.

Close to an hour later, her breathing changed, and she was struggling. I could see that it was happening in front of me. I could feel my heart break, my head spinning. My own breathing became short and quick. She was leaving, just as I had told her to. "Stop! I am not ready!" I cried out before she closed her eyes. I reached out and brought her into my arms, and she opened her eyes. Her breathing soothed, or rather, she continued as she had for weeks, taking short and shallow breaths.

I called the psychic to tell her what had happened. "Gracie is not going to go on her own!" she told me. "She is worried about you and her family." She agreed that I had stopped the process, and now it would take the hospice vet or Grace's health declining to the extent that her heart would stop before she could move on.

I believe in my heart that I held her back from moving on. Now as I look back at this moment, it brings me great pain. My heart still aches, knowing she was so worried about me that she stopped the natural process of her passing and stayed for me one more day.

CHAPTER 6

A DAY OF GRACE

The morning of Wednesday, September 23, arrived. I had nodded off on the sectional with Grace sleeping in the corner, Rico on the other end, and the kitties here and there as cats will do. I awoke to the phone at 8:00 a.m. It was a hospice vet's assistant saying that the doctor could fit us in that day. Dr. Ann was one of the hospice vets I had been trying to reach, and I got confirmation that she could be at my house at 3:00 p.m.—just in the nick of time, as Gracie's in-office visit had been scheduled for 5:00 p.m. This phone call set into motion a series of spiritual and cosmic events that continued for the rest of the day until I met with the psychic about thirty days later.

I was numb but felt the tears running down my face. I looked at Gracie and then at the rest of my clan. "Let's get it together," I told them, "because we are now down to hours, not days, for Gracie to be with us. The wheels are in motion." I looked at her. "I cannot stop it now, and unless you know of another way to keep this from taking place, it will happen." Then I went to the bathroom and washed my face, brushed my teeth, and changed my clothes. I was afraid to shower in fear that I might miss her exit.

I spoke to the other animals exactly as I am communicating with you now. "Today is going to be an awfully hard day for each of us, and we need to be available for Gracie. We need to show her the love we have for her, because we will not get another chance."

I looked at Grace, and we locked eyes. I spoke to her as if she were as human as my own being. "Gracie, I love you," I said to her. "I have loved you from the first second you walked into my life. You have been the most wonderful companion for Rico. You've been by his side every step of the way. You put up with Phoenix and his antics and gave him the attention he wanted from you while never once being mean to him. There were times he probably deserved it, but you never gave him anything but love.

"You have been a part of my family. I know you belong here with us, and I am your pet dad. I will always be your pet dad. I want you to know how much I appreciate you. I want you to know I adore you. I want you to know I love you and always will love you."

She looked at me as if she understood every word I spoke. I could see the love and compassion behind those eyes of hers. She didn't blink, only stared at me, and she didn't move. Then Gracie started to open her mouth, and it seemed like she was moaning a little, but in those moans, I heard words, sounds I heard as "I love you" and "Thank you" and "I'll miss you" and "I'll be waiting." The final was "I've always loved you, and thank you for saving me."

You are either having an incredible spiritual episode, I thought, *or you are losing your mind from pure exhaustion.* I heard what I needed to hear for my own comfort. Or who knows? I have never experienced anything like this from any other animal.

I told Gracie there were things I needed to say and apologize for before we ran out of time. I told her I was sorry I was about to do something that would end her life, but in my heart, I knew it was the right thing to do. She was in pain now, and I didn't want her to hurt. I held her head in my hands and sat on the floor so we could be at eye level. Eye to eye, I played one of my favorite songs for her. The lyrics go something like "I was there when you were a queen, and I'll be the last one there beside you." Gracie seemed almost to smile and relax a little with her breathing.

I repeated what the animal psychic had told me about her crossing. "Do not be scared. You know the way; you can do this!" But then I remembered the part that had bothered me and even hurt to think about. It would take her three days to cross to the other side. This wave of emotion came over me as I spoke to her again.

"Grace, this psychic tells me that it will take you three days to cross over to the other side. You won't be scared, and you know the way. But it really scares me that you will be on your own for three days, and I do not like the thought of you being alone without me! Not for three days! I can't protect you, honey, because I won't be there. I can't go with you, because if I do, I can't come back. Rico and the kitties need me here for their lives so I can protect and care for them too. I don't want you to feel like I am abandoning you, but this is how it works."

I had thought about it, and I told her I had an idea. "Gracie, whatever comes for you, whether it is an angel or angels, or this light we always hear about, or maybe even my own mom … whatever or whoever shows up for you—Gracie, I want you to run! You run away from here as fast as you can. It's okay to look back at us one last time and see all of us here in this room, and you might even want to stay. But don't. Take a good look at all of us, know how much we love you and will miss you, *and then you run to them*. Run to that light! I am telling you to run from here. Run, little girl, *run!*"

Then I thought maybe I should tell her what I knew about this moment to come. "Grace, when we die, we must give these bodies back. They are not ours to keep. They are on loan to us, and they belong to the earth. Maybe on the other side we will get new bodies. Bodies that won't ever be sick and are always young and, most importantly, will never die!"

I now believe that I was explaining this to Gracie so that *I* could get a better grasp on what was about to happen. Maybe saying it aloud would help with my own emotions, which were so very raw and vulnerable. I did not want her to feel or notice I was nervous and emotional. We are told by many animal experts that our animals notice our feelings and emotions and respond to them. I did not want her to experience the turmoil in my heart and my head.

Knowing that in a few hours she would be gone, I gave Gracie a bit of water from my fingers and wet her mouth, then picked her up and took her outside. I wanted to give her some fresh air and see if she could stand on her own. She could not. I carried her back inside and laid her gently on her blanket. Rico was on the sofa, and Grace used what strength she had left to pull herself across the sofa to be next to Rico. Watching this broke me down. It was the sweetest gesture she made in her last few moments. She wanted him to know how much she loved him. She was telling him goodbye.

CHAPTER 7
A GRACEFUL EXIT

Gracie was resting on the sofa, taking short quick breaths. She seemed comfortable, but I knew in my heart this was exceedingly difficult for her.

I opened all the windows and blinds in the family room, so it was very bright. I wanted to make sure Gracie could find a way out when she left. I had the TV playing in the background, one of our favorite shows that we all watched religiously every Sunday morning. I knew Gracie would feel comforted by hearing something familiar in the background.

I took out every memorial card I had of people I had loved and lost, the ones who had crossed over before us, and I arranged them on the entertainment center. I included a keepsake book of my dog Maxx, who had crossed over many years ago. Maxx had passed peacefully in his sleep at the age of thirteen. I put out a picture of my cat Cleo, who also passed in her sleep, at the age of twenty. There were a lot of cards and pictures up there. Far too many! I felt that by displaying so many of my ancestors, they would surely come and help her cross to the other side. I had to make sure she was not alone.

The phone rang. It was the hospice vet. She was five minutes away. I told her the front door was unlocked and to let herself inside. We were all in the back of the house in the family room. I had never met this doctor, so I knew only that she had a very soothing voice, and I could hear the compassion in her voice as she spoke.

It was close to 3:30 p.m. I looked at Gracie. "If you do not want this to happen, then you need to get up and walk around this room because I cannot stop this on my own. I need to know I am doing the right thing." She looked at me but didn't move. She didn't raise her head or even blink her eyes. I took that to mean she knew what was coming, and she was ready. Tears flowed steadily down my face, and my heart raced as I waited for the front door to open.

Within a few minutes I heard the door opening, and the vet called out my name. "Ron?"

"We are in the back room," I called out. "Please come on in. And shut the front door, please."

I did not look away from Gracie, but the other animals in the house were very leery and hyperaware. Rico barked at the vet and wouldn't stop. I think he knew who she was and what she was about to do. I saw the kitties walk up to her, but they wouldn't allow her to touch them. They moved away and out of sight for the moment. A stranger had just walked into our home—the one who would take Gracie out of pain but also away from us.

The vet asked how many pets I had. I found that odd. "Why?" She told me there were maybe seven to ten cats out on the front street and lawn. I looked out, and they were all feral, except for a few that belonged to the neighbors. I felt comforted as much as one can be in such a moment. It was as if the universe had put out a call so they could come for support. The universe, in all its wisdom and chaos, had summoned these creatures to my home for Gracie's last few moments. In this intense moment, the universe was trying to show us we were important; we were recognized. It was a feeling of pure awe!

The hospice vet introduced herself formally as Dr. Ann Smith. She said I could call her Dr. Ann. Dr. Ann was kind and had the look of someone who did a job, a complicated job, that few of us could or would do. I know I could not do this, not for millions of dollars a day. She looked as if she had been crying and told me she had just left another home with an extremely sick German shepherd, and the family was so upset. Rightly so, I thought.

Dr. Ann looked down at Gracie, remarked how beautiful she was, and asked if I was ready for this procedure to take place. I told her that I had never seen this done or participated in the euthanasia of any animal. It was my first time. Although I was nervous, I trusted her.

Dr. Ann began to explain the process and the exact steps she would take for Gracie. She started telling me about the two injections, but I stopped her and let her know we had been at this for quite a while now and were all worn out, especially Gracie. I asked if she could explain the procedure as it was happening. "Of course," Dr. Ann replied. She asked me to keep Gracie close to me and hold my hands on her body.

I put Gracie's head as close to mine as I could as I sat on the floor, gazing into her eyes. She was awake, but I could tell she was ready. She looked at me and fixed her eyes on me. I sensed she was telling me it was okay. Her eyes were wet. I didn't know dogs could cry, but it looked as if she were crying.

The vet said, "I am now putting a small tourniquet on her back leg, and I'm going to administer the relaxation injection. I want you to know this may take her life, because Grace is very close already, and I want you to be prepared." She told me this relaxation injection was more of a sedative but necessary before the next injection.

I looked at Gracie. "I love you," I said. "I am doing this because I love you." I motioned to the vet to go ahead with the injection.

I was aware of the other animals in the room. The cats were at the back screen door, which was open, and Rico had moved to the other end of the sofa. It felt like we were in slow motion. The relaxation injection was very evident when it flowed into Gracie's body. Her entire body became limp. Finally, she was able to relax. She seemed relieved, and I could see that her pain seemed to ease. She looked so calm, as if she had taken a huge breath and let it out.

The vet moved close and said, "Ron, I am about to give the last injection. This one will stop her heart. It may take a few seconds and could take up to three minutes. She will feel no pain. I want you to expect her mouth to open, and her tongue will protrude. Her eyes may roll back. Her heart will stop. She will stop breathing. She will feel no pain."

As I held on to Gracie, I asked the vet to let me know the very second her heart stopped. She readied her stethoscope. Her next words came slowly to my ears as if they were playing at the wrong speed. All I could hear her say was, "I'm releasing the medication, Ron."

I watched and held on to Gracie tightly. Her eyes rolled back, her tongue protruded, and her mouth was open. The vet placed her stethoscope over Gracie's heart. She looked at me and said, "She's gone." It only took a few seconds.

All I could say over and over was "No no no no no!" It felt like my heart had broken into a million pieces. I put my head on Grace's chest, and there was no noise. I kissed her little face. Dr. Ann had to help me up off the floor, and I saw her face. She was crying along with me, and I thought, *This woman, this wonderful woman, has the worst job in the world.*

I stopped crying for a minute and tried to compose myself. I had to let the vet know I was ready to get down to business. What is next, and how do I get her ashes and pay for this visit? I also wanted to make sure her cremation was private. Unless you ask for private cremation, animals are cremated together, I had learned when I researched the process on the internet. I wanted to make sure the ashes I received belonged to my Grace. These things I needed to ask, especially since this was a very new experience for me.

We stepped away from the sofa and walked about fifteen feet to the entertainment center. Dr. Ann asked about all the cards and pictures displayed there, and I told her about each of them and why I had them out.

While we stood and discussed the business aspects, something unusual happened. Phoenix, the youngest kitty in the family and Grace's favorite playmate, finally came from behind the sofa to sit at the back door of the family room. He had been close, waiting for this to be over. He walked very slowly around the sofa, instead of taking his usual path jumping over the back. Each step seemed more deliberate and calculated. He made his way to where Grace was lying. Dr. Ann nodded to me to watch him, and we both stood in silence and let him do what he needed to do.

Phoenix had not said his goodbyes to Grace, not that I was aware of, as the rest of us had. Now he was taking his turn. He positioned himself in front of Grace, hoisted himself up on his hind legs, and used his front paws to pull the folded blanket down so he could see her more clearly. He kept his paws on the blanket to keep it pulled down. His head turned side to side as if he were scanning her from head to toe. He did this several times and then locked his eyes upon her. He removed his front paws from the blanket. Then he lowered himself very slowly. After his paws were on the floor, he turned and walked away into the front living room, where the other two cats were waiting. He did not run. He walked as quietly as possible.

The vet was sobbing and said that if she hadn't witnessed this with her own eyes, she would never have believed it happened. Phoenix was saying his goodbyes and paying his last respects to his friend. He did so with the utmost dignity and humility. It was the purest form of love shown between two friends. This is a natural animal instinct, and it is called unconditional love.

After we both stopped crying, Dr. Ann asked if I had a blanket that I wanted to use to carry Grace to the car. I wanted to keep the blanket where she had rested, so the vet went out to her car and retrieved the blanket she had and brought it inside. I wanted to carry Grace out. My thoughts were, *I brought her into this house, and I will carry her out. And when the time is right, I will be the one to carry her back inside to her home.* The vet walked over to Grace and wrapped her so that she was secure.

Grace was wrapped with her head exposed. I walked over to where she was lying. I placed my hand under her head, and I lifted her to my chest and let her head rest on my shoulder. Her body was exceptionally soft and limp. I whispered into Grace's ear, "I kept my promise. I was the last one here beside you."

I walked slowly as I carried her though the house. In the front room, I passed each of her siblings, who watched me carry her. Once we were outside on the front porch, the vet noticed that my shoe was untied and reached down to tie my shoelace so I wouldn't have to put Gracie down. Then I carried Grace across my lawn to the vet's car. The rear hatch was open and ready. I laid Grace down inside. I took a deep breath, as if I were trying to memorize her smell. Dr. Ann told me she wished she could find a way to preserve their smell because so many of us do the same thing. I thought how heartbreaking it is that we will do anything in these last few moments to preserve those memories.

The veterinarian's office would contact me once Grace's private cremation was completed. When I was ready, I could come to the office to pick up her ashes, along with the footprints and other things I had requested in memory of Grace.

I know it's strange, but I asked the vet to drive away slowly. I don't know why. She pulled out of the driveway and drove down the street slowly at first then out of my sight.

As I turned to walk back to the house, the feeling was different. The house had changed. I felt an emptiness in the space. I noticed that among the cats who had gathered outside, a few lingered, but most of them were walking away. I do not know, but they seemed to know it was over, so it was okay to leave.

CHAPTER 8

MAKING IT KNOWN

Grace had taken her last breath at 4:02 p.m. EST.

Now it was time to alert my friends and family, especially the ones who had known Grace and loved her and helped take care of her. I knew I couldn't speak to anyone right then. I don't know if I could have spoken a single word. I felt drained. I texted my family and told them that Grace took her last breath, and she was gone. She was surrounded by her brothers and sisters, and the room was full of love. The windows were open so she could see a clear path out, and she went very peacefully. I thanked them for loving her and for caring about all of us. I wanted them to know first before I posted anything on social media.

Next, I sent a text to the animal psychic, the same information I sent to my friends. Her response was almost immediate. I have kept the text on my phone to this very day, reading it so many times that I have memorized it: *Thank you for telling me . . . . WOW! She moved quickly into the light, and she is already on the other side. Grace says thank you, she loves you, and she will tell you everything once you and I meet in the next month.*

I thanked her for guiding me though this and let her know I was looking forward to our meeting. I had so many questions swirling around my mind. I wanted to make sure Gracie hadn't experienced any pain when she took her last breath. I wanted to know who came for her and who she was with. I wanted to know if she saw us before she left.

Then I remembered the previous information from the psychic about the three days it takes to cross. But now she was telling me that Grace had moved into the light quickly! She was already on the other side. I wondered what had changed. Although I did not fully understand the circumstances or the message completely, I will admit it did bring me some peace at that moment. Just hearing from this woman telling me Gracie was on the other side took away some of the awfulness.

I sat in the front room with the rest of my clan, all of us looking out of the front windows. I think we were half-expecting Grace to come back into the house.

The phone rang. It was the other vet's office asking where we were. Were we still coming? With a lump in my throat and in my softest voice, I told them that Grace had crossed over about an hour ago and was already with her hospice vet.

Two days after Grace passed, the hospice vet called and left a voicemail. She was with Grace, and she was safe at the crematorium. This voicemail remains on my cell phone. I cannot bring myself to delete the message.

The next month was challenging for me and my little family. I spiraled in and out with many sleepless nights and lots of tears. I had panic attacks. I would wake up and relive the moment of her passing. I couldn't breathe! I would have to go outside into my front yard at two and three in the morning just to get air. I felt as if the house just wasn't big enough. Those panic attacks happened quite often over that thirty-day period.

Rico was acting differently too. He wasn't his usual happy peppy self. He slept a lot. He followed me from room to room, which he normally didn't do. The cats seemed distant. There were times when I went to pet them or show affection and they would pull away. I wondered if they were afraid of me because of what had happened to Gracie. Did they fear I was going to do the same thing to them? I'm probably exaggerating this, but I was so distraught I was grabbing at anything and everything to make sense of the loss of Grace.

I started grief counseling. I found out I had no idea how to process grief. The therapist told me to journal my emotions about the experience. That journal was the beginning of this book.

CHAPTER 9

A VISIT FROM THE PSYCHIC

I scheduled the animal psychic to come to my home on the last Sunday of October. I'd had a reading before, with a psychic in Los Angeles, and I knew that in order to get the full benefit of the visit, I needed to stay open-minded about the idea of a psychic and what she would have to say. I was anxious, nervous, excited, and yes, a little skeptical. I decided I would not divulge anything about the last few days with Grace, especially our last day. I would not tell the psychic anything about my talks with Grace or those last moments. I wanted the information to come from her and not from the things I said. I wanted to know what this woman could tell me, if she had communicated with Grace. What could she tell me about our last day and about Grace now?

The psychic arrived, and I introduced her to Rico and the kitties. She was kind and soft-spoken, and she sat on the floor so the animals could be closer to her. I appreciated that act of kindness. She seemed especially drawn to Rico.

I sat down on the floor with her. The only information I volunteered was Grace's location on the sofa. I had the memorial cards still out on display, and I opened the blinds just as I had done on her last day. Then I remained silent and let the psychic speak.

She spoke to Rico, which was fun to watch. She took his little head into her hand and tilted it upwards. He let her, surprisingly. She looked into his eyes. He sat on the floor with her and didn't move. Then the psychic said, "He hates his medicine because it tastes awful."

I had not told her that Rico has congestive heart failure and is on three different medications. But yes, he hates taking them, for sure. I nodded in agreement and smiled.

Rico

She met Duey and Izzy, and then Phoenix came into the room. She identified him at once as Grace's cohort and playmate. So far, she had been spot on, yet I remained quiet and stoic. I continued to let her speak.

Duey, Izzy, and Phoenix always ready for a photo op

She began to talk about Grace. She asked me who Gammy was. I did not know. She wondered if I had a grandmother who had passed. I did, but she was referred to always as Grandma, and I had known only one set of grandparents. The psychic asked about my mother. I replied that my mother had passed on many years before, when I was in my late twenties, and that none of her grandchildren called her Gammy, as they referred to her as Grandma or Mamaw. No Gammy here!

Then the psychic asked for a picture of my mom. I pointed to one displayed on the entertainment center. It had been taken of my mother standing in front of her favorite dogwood tree in the backyard of my childhood home. Mother was in her early sixties and extremely ill at the time.

The psychic looked at the picture and shook her head, saying, "No, that isn't Gammy." Then she noticed a picture of the woman who was like a second mom to me, my mother's closest sister and my favorite aunt. The psychic spoke about my Aunt Carrie for a few seconds. "This woman is remarkably busy cooking for hundreds and hundreds of people!" she said. She told me how happy my Aunt Carrie was to care for so many and asked if I might know why this would be true. I told the psychic that my aunt could not have children, and that is why we always thought of her as our second mother. I felt joy knowing my aunt was doing things she loved and caring for so many people!

"That fits," said the psychic, smiling. Then she began to describe the woman Grace was calling Gammy. "This woman is young," the psychic said, "with french braids or curls in her hair, and wearing ruby-red lipstick."

My heart was pounding. Among the photos on my phone was a picture of my mom taken when she was twenty-one years old. I took out my phone and scrolled to the photo. My mother, wearing a yellow dress, had blonde french braids and wore ruby-red lipstick! She had signed the picture with *Remember me always, Effie.*

My mother, age 21, in the photo that identified her as "Gammy"

As I turned over my phone to reveal the photo of my mother, the psychic instantly said, "That's her! Who is this woman?" I told her that this was my mother at age twenty-one. "This is Gammy, Ron," the psychic said. "This is who Grace is with, and she calls her Gammy."

All I could do was smile. I tried my best not to overreact as she spoke, but honestly, I was coming apart. I felt an instant bond again to my mother. My heart was full! My mother was now known as Gammy. And she had my Gracie with her!

The psychic began to speak about Grace in more detail. During the day, she said, before Grace had crossed, the "light" was here in the room. Not only once, but twice. The light had come to let Grace know it was ready for her when the time came. "She saw this light," the psychic told me, "and it was right behind you."

She asked if I had noticed anything that day. I could hardly speak to answer yes, so all I did was nod. I had noticed Grace look over my shoulders during the day as if she was seeing something behind me. I had turned but didn't see anything unusual. Apparently, Grace did. She was fixated on whatever was behind me.

The psychic continued. "Before I forget, Grace wants Rico to come to be with her, and she is always asking him to join her, but she also knows he isn't ready, and neither are you. Also, Rico does not want you to get another dog until he has crossed. He knows you will need one to help you process the loss of him, but for now he wants it to be just you and him."

She described how Grace's spirit had returned later that night, around eight o'clock, to check on us. She said that Grace had wanted me to see her for a moment. Grace knew, the psychic continued, that I wasn't doing well and was still having anxiety and crying. "Did you see her?" the psychic asked.

"Yes," I said, "over there around the staircase." Her image had been so real to me that I had got up from the sofa and called out her name, but by the time I made it to the stairs, she was gone. I knew I had seen her, but logic and my rational mind couldn't accept this as reality.

The psychic let me know that I was supposed to see her for only a second. Grace wanted me to see her in the house to show me that her spirit was alive and well and still with us.

Then we spoke about my sadness and the grief I was experiencing. I told her about a recent dream in which I saw Grace with my mom. In another dream, I was sitting at a bus stop crying, sobbing, tears flowing like rain down my face. The bus pulled up, and in the reflection of the bus's windows I saw myself, with Grace on my left side, standing on her hind legs licking the tears from my face.

"Grace is very worried about you," the psychic said, "but she wants you to let her go and live your life and take care of her siblings. She is telling you to let go of your sadness because you will meet again when the time is right."

I spoke to the psychic about the first conversation we had, when she had told me it takes three days for them to cross over. I showed her the text on my phone. Then I wanted to know why the message was so different on the day that Grace crossed. I read the words she had sent that day calmly but with a lump in my throat. " *'Wow! She moved quickly into the light, and she is already on the other side!'* What changed?" I asked. "What happened here? Why didn't it take her three days to cross?" I didn't say anything about what I said to Grace that day. Not a word!

Pausing for a moment, she took my hand in hers and looked up towards the sky. Then quietly she said, "Ron, you are a wonderful pet parent, and Grace says she was so lucky to have you, and she knows how much you loved her, and she will love you forever. But the thing that changed, my friend, is simple. The thing that changed on that day is that she did exactly as you told her to do … you told her to run! And she ran!"

AFTERWORD

After the psychic's reading, and she had left our home, I had time to reflect on the experience, the strange and unexplainable events, words, and spirituality in all that happened. Remembering that day brings me a feeling of reassurance and love. It was all love, all the time. It was as if the world stopped turning for just a moment, perhaps to let Gracie step off and make her way home. I cannot explain what happened. I cannot deny it either.

All I know, and what I feel, is that we have something extraordinary to look forward to when our lives end here on earth. We must continue to have faith that our energy, our memories, and the impressions we leave behind on the world are significant. Everyone and everything has the right to be here and be loved. We are born, and we take our place. We live our lives, and we hope we leave the world a better place than we found it. That we change someone for the better. That we give them hope or bring them joy. Or maybe just make someone smile. All the little things can make a difference. Even the smallest of things can bring about a positive change in someone's life—yes, even something as small and precious as a little rescue dog.

And now you know her story. The little dog that changed my life. And her name was Grace.

Printed in the United States
by Baker & Taylor Publisher Services